Manipulation

A Psychologist's Guide to Highly Effective Manipulation Techniques – Influence People with Persuasion, Mind Control, and NLP

or directions contained within is the solitary and utter responsibility of the recipient reader. Under no circumstances will any legal responsibility or blame be held against the publisher for any reparation, damages, or monetary loss due to the information herein, either directly or indirectly.

Respective authors own all copyrights not held by the publisher.

The information herein is offered for informational purposes solely, and is universal as so. The presentation of the information is without contract or any type of guarantee assurance.

The trademarks that are used are without any consent, and the publication of the trademark is without permission or backing by the trademark owner. All trademarks and brands within this book are for clarifying purposes only and are the owned by the owners themselves, not affiliated with this document.

Table of Contents

Introduction

Congratulations on getting a copy of *Manipulation: A Psychologist's Guide to Highly Effective Manipulation Techniques – Influence People with Persuasion, Mind Control, and NLP.*

The following chapters will discuss everything that you need to know to fully understand manipulation and how it works. All of us have experienced manipulation in some form or another in our lives. We may have had a time when our boss tried to convince us to stay late, when we saw an advertisement on television for something that we do not need, or when someone close to us tried to convince us to take a certain course of action. There were probably times when you tried to manipulate someone in order to get them to do something for you.

These types of manipulation are seen as relatively acceptable by society. However, when someone tries to take over the life of another person and does these techniques in a way to harm the other person, or at least in a way that shows that he or she does not care about the other person, it is seen as something entirely different. This guidebook will take a look at what is known as emotional manipulation and all the different components that come with it.

Inside this guidebook, we will take a look at some of the different parts of manipulation. We will look at how you can recognize it and who are the most likely targets of a manipulator. We will also discuss some of the ways that communication can help you to recognize and avoid manipulators in your life, and some of the techniques that you can use to make sure that you do not fall prey to a manipulator at some point in your life.

There are plenty of books on this subject on the market. Thanks again for choosing this one, please enjoy!

Chapter 1:
What is Emotional Manipulation?

All of us have been manipulated at one point or another. We may have let someone borrow our vehicle, get us to take on more work, or go on an outing that we were not looking forward to. This is part of life, and usually, because of our sense of obligation, we will do this without too much thought about it. There were probably times when you were able to manipulate others into helping you with something, whether or not they really wanted to. Not everyone wants to stay late at work, lend out their favorite shirt, or do something else with you, but because you use manipulation techniques (whether you know it or not), they are willing to do these things.

There is a difference between using manipulation to get a favor and using manipulation as a tool to always be in control of someone else. One common type of manipulation is known as emotional manipulation. Individuals who use this manipulation will play around with your emotions in a way that makes you feel bad or guilty if you are not doing the things that they want. Often, you can be in a relationship with someone where they try to manipulate you, which in turn can worsen the situation.

Everyone deserves to feel loved and valued. While they may get into a relationship where there are some disagreements and hard times, they both still have a mutual respect for each other, and both understand that there has to be some give-and-take in the relationship to make it work. This is the foundation of any good relationship. We may have times when we fall short of the ideal and we get angry or frustrated, or we may even use some passive-aggressive tactics to get our way during a disagreement. There are times when we may say a little white lie or throw out something hurtful towards the other person. So, how is this behavior different from what a manipulator does?

Basically, if you use some of those tactics and then feel guilty or regretful about them almost as soon as you do them, then you are likely not a manipulator. You may have used some of the techniques, but you did not intentionally mean to harm the other person. You likely did it because you were feeling hurt or angry at the time.

It is important to remember that all people are a little bit self-centered. But, those who are healthy and emotionally sound will recognize when this behavior comes out, and they will be able to make corrections to the behavior. They feel bad for acting this way and trying to use such horrible tactics to get the other person to do what they want. They may apologize and then work on coming to a solution that is more loving and will work for both parties. We all do or say things in anger or frustration that we do not mean, but it is how we react afterward that will determine if the actions are emotional manipulation.

What we described above is a healthy relationship. We recognize that sometimes the words out of our mouths are not the best, and we feel guilty right after we say them. However, there are those people in the world who are emotionally controlling and manipulative. They will use passive-aggressive behaviors to get their way, and they will keep using these behaviors to prevent you from saying or doing anything that they do not like. Many times, you may not even realize that the other person is using this kind of behavior because they are very good at deceiving you and keeping the information hidden. This often results in the victim leaving the situation a little bit confused on what happened.

On the other hand, there are some emotional manipulators who use more force and are more overt in their tactics. They will use tactics that will leave you shamed, in fear, or they utilize guilt trips, and often the victim will be left feeling immobilized and stunned. This is exactly what the manipulator wants them to feel. If the victim is stunned and not able to respond to them, they can walk away as the winner, and in their eyes, that is enough.

Either way, emotional manipulation can mess with the mind of the victim. The longer the victim is exposed to this, the more confidence and power the manipulator will gain, and the better they become at manipulating. This kind of manipulation can easily destroy a relationship because all the respect, intimacy, and trust will crumble. This is true whether this kind of manipulation is occurring in an intimate relationship, a professional relationship, or other kinds of relationships.

Signs that someone is emotionally manipulative

There are a number of signs that you can look for when it comes to finding out if you are being manipulated by an emotional manipulator. Some of these signs include:

- *They can make you question things:* You will find that emotional manipulators are very good at lying. They will insist on saying that an incident did not happen, despite evidence to the contrary, or that they never said something that you remember them saying. This manipulator is a good liar. So good, that you begin to question your sanity in the process.

- *The actions do not match the words:* Emotional manipulators are good at telling you what you would like to hear, but the actions they perform will say a different story. For example, they will say they support you, but when it is time to help you out, they will act like the requests you make are unreasonable. Or, they will say that they are lucky to know you but then turn around and act like you are a big burden to them.

- *Hand out the guilt trip:* Emotional manipulators are good at using guilt against you. So, if you ever bring up that something is bothering you, they will be able to turn it around and make you feel guilty that you even mentioned it. With these manipulators, whatever you do is wrong, and everything is always your fault, no matter what.

- *They are always the victim:* No matter what, the manipulator is never the one to blame. It does not matter what they do or fail to do, they can always blame someone else, and that someone else is usually going to be you. If you get upset at them for this, they will blame you for having unreasonable expectations. If they get mad, then it is all your fault because you got them upset. These individuals are not able to be accountable for anything.

- *They suck you into their emotions:* No matter what emotion these individuals are feeling, they will share it with everyone around them. These are the people who, if they are in a bad mood, then everyone near them will know as well, and it is likely that everyone else will feel it, too.

- *They are eager to help, and then play the martyr:* They may seem like they are on board to help out with whatever you need, but this is quickly followed by a lot of sighs, groans, and suggestions that what they are doing is a big burden. If you tell them that they do not need to help or you can do it on your own if it is too big of a deal, they will turn it around and say that, of course, they want to help, and you are just being paranoid. The goal of this is to make you feel guilty and even a little bit indebted to them.

- *They are the masters of the one-up:* No matter what you are dealing with in life, the emotional manipulator has it so much worse. They will undermine your legitimate complaints by constantly reminding you that their problems are more serious. The message here is that you do not have a reason to complain, so just be quiet.

As you can see, the emotional manipulator can change a lot of things so that you feel either sorry for them, responsible for them, indebted to them, or there is something seriously wrong with you. They can often do this in a subtle manner, so that over the years, you are slowly becoming more in debt to them and more manipulated. This is one of the hard parts of manipulation. It is often going on so long that you are not sure how to fix it once you have figured out what is going on.

Chapter 2:
Identifying Hidden Manipulation

There are different types of manipulation that you will encounter during your life. When we are talking about covert manipulation, we are talking about a kind that occurs under the level of your conscious awareness. If you are a target of this type of manipulation, you probably will not be aware of what is going on, which makes it the most difficult type of manipulation to spot and deal with.

Some of the most skilled manipulators will be able to make you doubt your emotional well-being and self-worth, which makes it easier for them to be able to control you. When you fall into this trap, the manipulator is then able to take away your identity and a lot of your self-esteem. This does take a lot of time to accomplish, but then they have time to get you to do what they want.

Most experts will refer to these skilled manipulators as covert-aggressive people. They will have a tool belt of tactics that they can use to get their target to do their bidding. And, they are usually so skilled at what they do that the target will fall prey without ever noticing. Some of the tactics that a covert manipulator will use includes:

- The ability to hide their aggressive intentions,

- Make you afraid, make you doubt yourself, and more, until you are willing to concede or give in to them.

Dangerous manipulators

Good emotional manipulators can use almost any type of behavior to accomplish their goals. They are even more dangerous when they can read behavioral patterns and the actions of their target. When they can read their target, they will soon know their target inside and out, such as their level of conscientiousness, weaknesses, fears, insecurities, and beliefs. And in the hands of a manipulator, knowledge is power that they can use against their target.

In some cases, the manipulator can even become known as a psychopath. There are many manipulators who do not fall into this category, but still, manipulators are really hard to have real relationships with. They will take a lot of time to study people, and then they will never think twice when they use that information against their target. They are more concerned about being able to get what they want in every situation that they will not stop to consider their target's feelings or how they should be acting in a real relationship.

One factor that you need to keep in mind is that manipulators have a need to be in control. They are power hungry, and they will do whatever they need to achieve that goal. They will often hurt people in the process, and it will not bother them at all. If you ever feel that you are less superior, less intelligent, less strong, or less confident in your life, especially if you are around a specific person, then this person may be manipulating you.

Think about the relationship that you are in right now. Are you able to remember back when you first met them? Was it something magical, something that swept you off your feet? You will find that most manipulators are sweet talkers. They are experts at being able to hide their real personalities and real plans from their target. They already have plans to trick you to get what they want, and they will start from the first moment that they meet you.

In the beginning, this person will make you believe that they are willing to do anything for you, and they will keep up with this act until you are hooked deeply, and until you show them your vulnerability. Once you have done this, they will start to bring out the manipulation, and sometimes the extreme abuse will start if you let it.

Over time, usually pretty slowly, so it is hard to pinpoint when it actually started, you will be able to notice that your ideal relationship has changed. It has become more confusing, exploitative, and demeaning. You will notice that the self-esteem that you had in the beginning (whether it was strong or not) will start to turn into doubt, and it is likely that you will start to blame yourself for this issue.

At this time, the manipulator will have full control. It will not be long until you are fine with just getting crumbs out of all the interactions in the relationship. You will be blamed for everything that goes wrong, even if you had nothing to do with it. You will have to take care of all their needs and care about them all the time, while they will no longer care about you or your fears, needs, and emotions. These manipulators do not really care about any of these things; they only pretended to care in the beginning to get you hooked on them.

It is amazing how quickly things can change. Once a target is under the control of their manipulator, even those with very high self-esteem will turn it around. They will start to blame themselves for anything and everything that goes wrong in their relationship. They will start to over analyze things that happen in their lives, and usually, they will do this until they are so confused that they do not know what is going on in their lives. Every part of their day can start to suffer because of this confusion and the tactics of the manipulator such as their mental health, physical health, social relationships, and career.

The sad part about all of this is that the manipulator will be able to do all of this without you seeing where it started. It is not something that happens one day, and then you can see it and leave. It starts out slowly, usually with a few little remarks or tactics that are used. Then one day, the manipulator will have taken over all the control, and you don't know how to handle the issue at all or to understand what is going on.

Chapter 3:
Manipulators and Targets

Now, while all of us will try to manipulate another person on occasion to help us get things done or to get something else we want, not everyone is easily manipulated. Sure, you could probably get someone to give you a ride on occasion, but that does not mean that you would be able to do some of the emotional and covert manipulative techniques that we talked about on them. There are some types of people who are more susceptible to being manipulated, who make the job of the manipulator easier, and these people will often find that they are not pulling the strings at all in their own lives.

So, how do you know if you are a prime target for a manipulator? Could you be one of those people who manipulators are looking for all the time? Some of the people who can be easily manipulated include:

- *Those who rely on others for information:* If you rely on someone else for information, you are just asking for someone to try and fool you. You have to be alert to the things that are going on around you, and you have to learn to make informed decisions that use common sense. Otherwise, a manipulator will quickly take over, and you will just go along with them because it is the easiest path.

- *Those who do not think through their decisions:* For those who like to think quickly, a manipulator is helpful to them. The manipulator can come in and help them make the decision. Someone who thinks through their decisions will not like the idea of someone else coming in and trying to do the work for them. But those who want to get the decision-making over with quickly will appreciate the help that the manipulator will give.

- *Those who have low self-confidence:* Those who have low self-confidence are perfect targets. These individuals often are overlooked by others and may not have a lot of friends. The manipulator can come in and offer to be that friend and can work to build up the confidence of their target. As they are doing this, the target will feel indebted to the manipulator and will be more likely to do what the manipulator wants.

- *Those who respond to guilt:* Guilt can be a powerful motivator, and a good manipulator will be able to use this to their advantage. These targets want to be helpful and do not want to feel guilty for not doing something that they should. A manipulator can play the victim card a little bit with this one, and they are sure to get this target to act the way that they want.

- *Those who like flattery:* If you are someone who likes to listen to flattery and will chase it down, then you will be a very easy target for a manipulator. All the manipulator will need to do in this situation is start adding in some flattery. They could spend time with you, compliment you often, and just be overall nice to you. These actions will stroke your ego, and you will open yourself up to do what the manipulator wants.

- *Those who are empathetic to others:* This is a great option to go for as a manipulator. These people like to help out others and are always falling for the next sob story they hear. They understand that people fall on hard times, and they want to be there to help.

While their ideals may be altruistic, many people will take advantage of this. They simply need to make the target feel bad for them, such as telling them a sad story or letting them know that they, the manipulator, is used to this abuse. If they can do this properly, this kind of target will jump into helping them right away.

- *Those who become blinded by love:* Manipulators love this kind of target because they will be able to make them fall deeply in love. They will say and do all the right things to make the target believe that they are in love. The target believes that they are so much in love that the other person would never harm them.

While it is possible for anyone to be manipulated during their lives, there are some people who are easier targets than others. If you fall into one of the categories above, it may be time to make some changes before someone tries to manipulate you and take over your life. Remember that the manipulator is not willing to work harder than they need to manipulate the other person. If they feel that someone will be at least a little bit difficult to manipulate, they will pick someone else to target.

You can't change your manipulator

It is impossible to change your manipulator, and trying to do this is just going to result in heartache and more issues in your life. However, you can make changes in yourself that will make things more difficult for the manipulator and perhaps make them go away.

The moment that you stop pleasing, complying, or cooperating with the manipulator is the moment that they will leave you alone. The manipulator does not want to work hard for the control, and if you start putting up a fight, then they will take off and look for someone else.

There are many targets who believe that they can change their manipulator. They want to stay around in the hopes that the manipulator will suddenly realize what is going on and will want to make a change. However, this is never going to happen. While there may be a few manipulators who are unaware of the tactics that they are using, most manipulators are skilled at what they are doing, and they have been working for a long time to perfect their techniques. These individuals will be impossible to change. Even when they are confronted and made aware of how they are hurting the target, they will not find the motivation to change.

Most manipulators can disguise their motives by hiding behind a lot of layers of lies. It is impossible to add on all these layers without knowing exactly what you are doing, and it is unlikely that they care that you think it is a bad thing. As long as they can maintain the control, they will be happy.

Since there are all these layers of lies that the manipulator has to maintain, they will often use some tactics that are considered acceptable by society. This can just make it more confusing for the target. Some of the tactics that they may consider using include:

- The manipulator will resort to caring for and loving their target for a time. They will spend some time showing the target how much they care for them. They use this love as a bargaining tool to get the target to do what they want.

- The manipulator may try to overpower the target, sometimes making the target feel like the manipulator is the expert.

- The manipulator can try to show the target how generous they are. They will show the target that they care because they are helping them out in any way they can. They may say that they are doing something to help out the target, or they are doing it for the target's own good.

One thing that you should consider is that it is not a good idea to ask a manipulator what their true intentions and motives are. You are not going to get an honest answer at all. The manipulator is a skilled liar, and they will be able to keep it all hidden. Often these questions will result in the manipulator getting defensive or angry towards you. Most manipulators have the idea that they deserve to do these things because they help them get to their goals, no matter what it takes.

Chapter 4:
Why Do You Behave the Way You Do?

Every person you talk to will have their own perception of things. You can get five people to watch the same thing happen, and they will all describe it in a different way. What you personally believe is wrong, could be the right thing for someone else. It is how the mind works, and there is not much that you will be able to do about it. Sometimes though, when you get frustrated with someone who does not seem to understand what you want from them, or when you can't figure out why someone you are close to is acting differently, then you may want to know exactly why people do the things they do.

It is important to realize that people have their own minds. Everyone is different, and you are not going to find two people who are exactly alike. Even when you run into twins, you will find that they will have very different views on the world and different personalities. There are many reasons why people may be different. It could be things like their culture, their gender, their environment, their thoughts, feelings, habits, emotions, and more.

We all have different motivations

You will find that there is an unwritten rule in actions and behaviors, and that is that all people will act based on the things that motivate them. People will act and do things in a different way because there are differences in what they need and want. Each person may choose to use different strategies to attain these needs and wants.

Now, there is no right or wrong answer here, mainly because most people will have their own concept of what is right for them. It is all about the perception. People do have the same core needs, which means that while personalities might change on the surface, everyone starts out in the same boat. It is also possible that there will be more than one of these basic human needs that can motivate you, which means there are many reasons for the actions that you complete. Each person may have similar core needs, but we can still have varying degrees of awareness when it comes to the relationship between our actions and our needs.

When you are not aware of the things that you need, you may start actions based on your feelings, your impulses, habits, and thoughts. Each of these types of motivation can be a reason to take responsibility for the choices that you make. Everything that you do will connect back to your needs, and you will continue on with this without thinking about what you are doing.

Our thoughts and feelings

There are many times when we will do things simply because we feel that we had to do them. In addition, we may do things because our emotions, such as satisfaction, joy, and happiness will lead us to do things because we want to feel these emotions. In addition, there are times when we will want to avoid certain things because we want to avoid some of the negative feelings, such as shame, guilt, and fear.

Feelings, in humans, are immediately going to be translated into action, and often this will happen without truly understanding what is wanted. Most of the time, the feelings will give a more commanding action so that you will just take action rather than first thinking about and trying to understand the action that is behind it. So, if someone can play on your emotions, such as working on your fear or your need to be liked and wanted, they are more likely to get you to act the way that they want, even if you do not fully understand why you are acting that way.

Understanding the brain

Our brains are pretty complex. We have two parts that come together to make us who we are. We have the more complex parts that may be newer among mammals but allow us to have rational thoughts. But, then we have the limbic system that forms the emotions and how we should react to the things that are going on around us. Both of these help to make us modern humans, but they are sometimes going to make us react in ways that we do not fully understand.

Essentially, to build up the emotional intelligence (EQ) that we need, we must have effective communication between the rational brain and the older and more primitive emotional structures that come with the limbic system. This is known as neuroplasticity, and it is basically the process of forming new neural pathways in the brain in response to learning new things.

You can use a variety of strategies to develop your own EQ levels in the same way. When you use these strategies, you are working to strengthen the billions of neuron pathways that are found in the brain. This will also allow those pathways to branch out and form connections with the cells that are nearby, which will improve your cognitive ability.

As this process continues to expand, it will essentially increase the rate of positive feedback loops and will ensure that anything that you practice on a regular basis will be habitual in nature, making it easier to perform in the future.

As you can imagine by this, there will be a large separation between the thinker and the feeler in each person, and both of these have the ability to pull you in different directions. This is what will leave many people open to manipulative behavior, especially if the thinker and the feeler inside are not aligned properly.

Your feelings are the things that will compel you to do things from within, while your thoughts will compel you to do things from without. This is an important thing to remember because it can show the freedom of being able to choose rather than being compelled to do something.

When it comes to making a choice, that choice is always going to be internal. The individual will be able to decide whether they will do something or not. For most individuals, they will take into consideration what consequences will occur from their actions before they make any decisions. There is a difference between believing that you need to do something, and choosing things based on what is important.

So, you will see that your thoughts will contain a variety of information about many things that you hold important and can be an expression of your needs. There are those who do not have a vibrancy of feeling. Those who are better able to manage their feelings are simply those who have more control over these feelings.

How can a manipulator step in?

At this point, you may be wondering how the manipulator can step in and use this to their advantage. Remember we talked about how when you learn a new skill, your neurons can form new paths that get stronger the more that you practice? This skill can be anything from learning how to bake something for dinner to learning how to behave in church.

The manipulator will use this to their advantage. They will slowly be able to teach you the way that you should behave. They may suggest a certain course of action, and if you do not follow it, they will start to do actions that will train your brain to behave the way that they want, and they will utilize your emotions to help make that connection stronger than ever.

Let us say the manipulator does not want you going out with friends at night because they want you to instead hang out with them and make dinner. You may fight this a few times and say you want to go out and see friends anyway. They can then resort to the fear emotion, yelling at you and demeaning you. Any time that you decide you want to go out with friends, they will start up with the yelling and fighting. Any time that you agree to stay home, they will pick another emotion, such as love. Your brain will quickly catch on to this pattern, and you are more likely to do what the manipulator wants to avoid the fear and receive the love.

This is just one example of how a manipulator can use the workings of the brain against you. They are usually able to do it in such a covert way, and over enough time, that it becomes hard for the target to know what is going on or how to make it all stop.

Chapter 5:
Am I Being Manipulated?

In truth, it will be very hard for you to know whether you are being manipulated or not. Manipulators know that as soon as you figure out what they are up to, the game is over. They need to keep this information hidden from you as much as possible, or they are not likely to get their way any longer. It is possible that you are already dealing with manipulation in your life without really realizing it at all.

However, if you have started to look around and notice that things are not right, it can be a scary time. The manipulator is good at what they do, and they will be able to hide a lot of this from you. How are you to know whether you are being manipulated or not? This chapter will take a look at some of the signs that you can look for to determine whether you are being manipulated or not. Sometimes, there may be more than one of these signs present in your life.

- *They bring you to home court:* The manipulator will often take you to some place where they can have the upper hand. This could include their office or their home, so that they are the one in charge.

- *Allows you to speak first:* They will do this to feel you out and find where your weaknesses are. They may ask a lot of questions, and they will be able to use that information about you.

- *Changing the facts to benefit themselves:* A good manipulator can change the facts to suit themselves. They will often lie and make up excuses so that you are the offender and they are the victim in any situation. They can add in exaggerations, and often they will withhold information that is important to make you look crazy. They can also change the situation around so that you turn out to be someone who can't be trusted.

- *Resort to intellectual bullying:* There are people who will take advantage of their target by imposing alleged statistics and facts that the target does not have much knowledge about. This can happen in sales and negotiations, as well as in personal arguments. The manipulator will use this to make you feel that they are the expert, and then they will keep going to sway you over to their agenda without you knowing what is going on.

- *Expose your weaknesses:* The moment that you show you have a weakness to a manipulator, they will take these weaknesses and use them against you. They will highlight these weaknesses and then turn around and show you that they will be the strength. This is the beginning of them being able to control you because they are leading you to feel that you need them when you do not. They may make humiliating comments about your appearance, belittle your background, flag you when you run late, or speak out about how bad your last project was. They are experts at being able to make you look bad while making themselves look great.

- *Using a tone of voice to overwhelm you:* One way to tell that you are being manipulated is when the other person consistently raises their voice during disagreements as well as during simple discussions. This is known as aggressive manipulation. They will often make their tone of voice loud enough that you will give them what they want, and then they will add some strong body language to make their point stronger.

- *Negative surprises*: Skilled manipulators can use some negative surprises as a method to distract you while they are trying to gain their advantage over you. A red flag that this is going on is that the negative information will be revealed without any warning because this makes it hard for you to think ahead and prepare for the surprise.

- *Leaving you with no time to decide:* This is when you are in a discussion with the manipulator, and then when you are trying to decide on something, they will put on a lot of pressure to make you decide right then and there. They can often talk about how time is important, and they can apply a lot of tension on you to get the result that they want.

- *Judgmental words and criticisms:* Manipulators are not known to mince their words, and they will often make critical remarks that are disguised as sarcasm or playfulness. This is done to make you feel inferior to them. Often this criticism will be over something trivial, but it will make a big difference to the target and can put the manipulator in control.

- *Using the silent treatment:* Skilled manipulators will give you the silent treatment. They will choose not to answer your emails, texts, and calls for some time. They will overpower you in this way because they will make you wait and feel in doubt about things. Their silent treatment will be the leverage that they need because it will add some uncertainty to your mind.

- *Playing dumb:* There are some manipulators who will resort to being ignorant in many situations. They will try to appear like they have no idea what you want or what you are asking them to do. They will make you take on the responsibility, and they will make sure that you have to work hard for it. This is a technique that manipulators will use to avoid responsibilities and obligations.

- *Guilt-baiting:* Manipulators can target your soft spot and will resort to blaming that is not reasonable. They will make sure that you are responsible for their happiness, which makes it easier for them to ask for unreasonable requests and demands at any time.

- *Playing the victim:* It is likely that a manipulator will play victim to get what they want. They will tell about exaggerated health and personal issues, and most of these will be imagined issues. They will show off how frail they are, how no one is there to help them out, how no one cares about them, and so on. This will make the target feel bad for the manipulator, and they are more likely to do what the manipulator wants.

- *Using emotional blackmail:* This person will work on your emotions to get you to do what they want. If you are with someone who threatens to kill themselves if you are making them mad or will not do what they want, it is likely that you are in a manipulative relationship.

- *Using the foot in the door strategy:* This is a scary one to work with because it starts out small and will build up without the target understanding what is going on. The manipulator will start out by asking for something small. When you agree to it, they will then follow up with the real request that they want. This puts the target in a tight spot because it is now hard for them to say no. If the target is not willing to do the real request, the manipulator will hurt the target making them feel like the bad one in the relationship. When you try to defend yourself, the manipulator will know that it will not take long to get you to agree to what you want.

- *Using humor and jokes:* A manipulator will make you feel embarrassed and intimidated whenever you are with them or with someone else as well. Then, when someone tries to confront the manipulator about what they are doing, the manipulator will declare that it was just a joke and that you should not take things so seriously. Most people will then shrug it off, but it works as a manipulative technique.

As you can see, there are a lot of different tactics that the manipulator will be able to use against their target. The manipulator is good at being able to do all of this without the target even knowing what is going on. But if you are in a relationship with someone, and you notice a few of the tactics above, it is likely that you are working with a manipulator.

Chapter 6:
How to Master Nonverbal and Verbal Communication

People in our modern world are constantly communicating with one another all of the time. Whether it is speaking with someone you know, using your body language, or sending out a text or email, it is likely that you are communicating with someone at all times of the day. While everyone will spend much of their lives communicating, it is the manipulators who are the ones who have above average skills in the communication department.

When it comes to communication, there are two aspects that you need to be aware of. These include nonverbal communication and verbal communication. Let us take a look at each one of these and how they are used when you want to deal with the people around you effectively.

What is verbal communication?

First, we will take a look at verbal communication. This is what you most likely thought about when we first brought up the idea of communication. Verbal communication will be anything that involves words, whether you are working with spoken words, written words, or even sign language. The conversation that you had with your spouse as you headed out the door can be verbal communication, the newspaper that you read, and the text message that you read at work.

Your ability to communicate a specific language will depend on more than just the sounds that you are making, but also the organized system of words. This is what sets humans apart from one another, even when we are talking about a distance between each other.

So, why is verbal communication so important? It is actually an integral part of our lives because it is the main way that we can communicate and express ourselves, as well as the thoughts and feelings that we have. We can use this kind of communication to inform people, whether to share information, communicate our needs, or to do something else.

Clarification is one crucial component that comes with verbal communication. There will be some individuals who are considered more articulate than others, while some will have difficulties when they try to express themselves in the spoken word. However, if you never use verbal communication with others, it will result in a lot of misunderstandings along the way.

What is nonverbal communication?

Nonverbal communication is very interesting to study. It is all the things that you say without using any words. It will include your body language, such as your eye contact, your posture, gestures, and even facial expressions. The sound of your voice can even be a large part of your nonverbal communication and will include things like the volume, pitch, and tone.

There are many instances when the meaning behind the words a person says will be completely different than the literal translation. For example, sarcasm would be impossible if you were not paying attention to the pitch and tone of voice of the other person. Your clothing choice can even be a part of what you can communicate with others without using your words, and it is often the basis of opinions that others have for you.

When you are speaking with someone and you would like to know what their real intentions are, it is important to look at the things that they are not saying, because while the person may be able to lie to you, their body language will not be able to lie.

According to some studies, there is a lot more that is said through body language and nonverbal communication than the words that are being said. Some facts about the relationship between nonverbal and verbal communication include:

- Seven percent of messages that pertain to feelings and emotions will come from the actual words that the person says.

- Thirty-eight percent will come from the paralinguistic element. This basically means that the meaning will come from the way that the words are spoken.

- The rest will come from the facial expressions and the other parts of body language.

So, you can easily see how important these gestures and nonverbal elements can be when you are communicating with others.

Mastering communication

While all of us spend a lot of our lives communicating with other people, it is important to work on your skills a little bit more. When you learn these skills, you will be able to use them to better discern the intentions of other people. These skills will help you to hide your weaknesses better, so it is less likely that a manipulator will be able to take advantage of you.

Verbal communication

First, we will take a look at your verbal communication and some of the things that you need to pay attention to when you want to make sure you are mastering communication. Some of the aspects that you need to consider include:

Your vocabulary

The words that you choose to communicate with will be important tools when you are working with verbal communication, so you need to choose what you say wisely.

Words can be very powerful because they can help to put you in a position of power. If a person is using rudimentary vocabulary, then you should make sure that you are sticking with language that is simple as well. However, if you can tell that they have a larger range of diction, you can match your vocabulary to theirs.

When you have a wide lexicon, you can tune your communication, and this will make it easier to draw people into you. A skilled manipulator who has a rich vocabulary can use that to their advantage. You will find that if you are limited in vocabulary, you will be more likely to fall prey to the manipulator, so consider expanding the words that you know and use.

Tone and pace

While working on your vocabulary and trying to increase it are important if you want to be able to beat out a manipulator, you need to make sure that others can understand what you are saying. The pace that you use while you speak can say a lot about you. If you talk too fast, it means that you are really excited about something. However, if you choose to speak at a slower pace, it may mean that you want to speak in a way that is easier for the other person to understand.

You should also consider the volume of your voice. It is easier to get the audience to listen to what you are saying if you use a voice that is clear and loud. It is also good to work on your projection so that you can shift the volume of your voice when it is needed.

Enunciation

Finally, you will find that enunciation is an integral part of the whole process of verbal communication. When you can clearly enunciate your words, it will give you an edge over everyone else. You should make sure that you can clearly enunciate your words to avoid issues with miscommunication and misinterpretation.

Nonverbal communication

There are also a few different parts of nonverbal communication that you should work on. When you can master these, you are more likely to get your message across and show that you are confident in the things that you are doing and saying. Some of the aspects of nonverbal communication that you should focus on include:

Hands

Hand gestures can be very important when you are communicating. You will be able to tell a lot about the other person by observing how they use their hands. People will often use their hands to emphasize an idea or to prove their point. Overall, the hands and the arms can be a defensive barrier, or they can show either an openness or a security when they are in a neutral position by the side of the person. On the other hand, they can show insecurity and apprehension when the person crosses them in front of the chest.

It is important that you learn how to properly use your hands to showcase your information to the other person. Hand gestures can be nice to use, but you do not want to go overboard and turn the other person off. If you would like to show yourself as an open and welcoming person, you should make sure that your hands are not folded or crossed right in front of you.

Eyes

Your eyes can help you out so much when it comes to your nonverbal communication. Not only do you use your eyes to take in the world around you, but they can also help you to figure out what the other person in the conversation is thinking or feeling.

When you are doing nonverbal communication, you need to make sure that you maintain a good amount of eye contact. When it comes to manipulation though, you should be more concerned with how the eyes are moving. You really want to take a look at the direction the eyes of the other person are going if you want to know what they are thinking or feeling.

For the most part, a person will look to one side when they are being asked a question. When they are reflecting on something, they will look either to the left or to the right. The side that they look to will often relate to the side of the brain that they are accessing. The right side will be concerned with creativity and the emotions, and the left side will be the direction when they are dealing with facts and figures.

Overall, if you are talking to someone, and they keep looking to the right, it means that they are trying to tap into the creative part of their brain. Often, this means that they will fabricate a story. This is not a big deal if you are asking them a question, and they respond with something like, "I do not know, but I imagine it would be..." Here, they are being honest with you and not stating things as facts when they do not know the answer.

However, if you are talking to someone, and they look to the right, and they say something like, "I dealt with something like that last week, and this is how we handled it," then you are dealing with something that is much more worrisome. This is because the person is stating something as truth, but they are responding in a way that means they are using the storytelling part of the brain. This is not always going to hold true, but if someone is using that part of the brain, it is likely that they will be making up a story to use.

To find out more, you also need to pay attention to whether the person is not only looking to the right but also if they are looking up or down. If the person is looking to the right and downwards, it means that they are looking more at the emotional part of their creativity. They may simply be recounting the feelings that they have had regarding that situation rather than making up an answer.

However, if you ask a question and the person looks to the right and up, then this could mean that they are fully accessing the imagination centers of their brain, and it is likely that they are making up a story as a response to your question.

If you are talking to someone and they are looking to the left, then it is more likely that they are trying to access the memory centers of the brain, and they are telling the truth. This is especially true when the person is not only looking to the left, but they are looking upwards. This means that they are likely getting their information from the image and memory centers of the brain and it makes it more likely that they are telling you something truthful. If the person is looking to the left and then down, it also indicates that they are being honest because they are using rationalization before they answer.

Position and posture

Communicators who are confident in themselves will stand up straight and command authority. They will not slouch, and they will be able to speak with authority. If you can do this all of the time, it is not likely that a manipulative person will see you as a target. Always make sure to watch what your posture and position are saying about you to other people. When you can stand up straight and tall, it shows other people that you have a lot of confidence and that you are not one to be taken advantage of.

As you can see, there are a lot of different parts that come with communication. It is not all about the words that you tell to another person or that you write down. It is also about the way that you say the words, how you make eye contact, how you can maintain the right posture and position, and how you use your hand gestures. Make sure to learn how to use all the different types of communication, both the verbal and the nonverbal, to help you to keep manipulators away and to recognize when you are dealing with a manipulator.

Chapter 7:
What is NLP?

When you are born, you have the same neurology as everyone else. Our ability to be able to do anything in our lives, whether that means cooking a great meal, reading a book, or being able to run very fast will depend on how we are able to control our nervous systems. When it comes to NLP, or neuro-linguistic programming, we are learning how to think more effectively while also communicating better with others as well as ourselves. Let's take a look at some of the different parts that come with NLP:

- Neuro: This is all about your neurological system. NLP is based on the idea that we are able to experience our world with our senses, and then we are able to translate that information through unconscious and conscious processes. Thought processes are able to activate the neurological systems, which will then be able to affect our behavior, emotions, and physiology.

- Linguistic: This part refers to how we are able to use our language to make sense of the world around us. When we are talking about NLP, it is the study of how the words we use will influence our experience.

- Programming: This comes from different types of pattern behaviors that are learned from experience. Your personal programming will consist of the internal processes and strategies that you choose to use in order to evaluate, learn, make decisions, and solve problems. With NLP, you will be able to recode your experiences and then organize your internal programming to make sense of the world around you.

The NLP Communication Model

The communication model of NLP is based on a cognitive psychology. According to this model, when someone behaves in a specific way, a chain reaction is going to be set up within you, which will then cause you to respond in some way. Then this reaction will create a reaction in the other person, and this goes back and forth.

This is something that you may see happening when you work with a manipulator, and they are able to use this to their advantage. They know that their reaction to something is going to influence the way that you see things. If they turn something into a big deal, then you are more likely to react to it as a big deal also.

Our internal thinking can greatly influence the way that we are able to perceive the world. Sometimes we see the world in a great light, or we see ourselves with great self-esteem. It is hard to change our outlook on things because we have used NLP to help us feel good. It is not likely that the manipulator is going to come and attack you if you have this positive outlook.

But if you are always nervous about what is going on in your world, your filter is not that good, or you are not using NLP properly, then it is likely that the manipulator is able to come around and use it on you.

If you feel that your outlook on things is changing or you start to react as a mirror of the other person, it is likely that the manipulator is using these techniques to help you out. The manipulator is able to work with all parts of this process, including changing the way that you make decisions and problem solve, and you have to be able to stop them as much as possible.

If you use NLP properly, though it takes some time, and you may need some professional help if you have been dealing with a manipulator who has been using NLP against you, you will be able to recode your experiences and organize your internal programming. This helps you to get some better outcomes than what the manipulator is trying to use against you. But if the manipulator is able to use the information against you, then you will be able to use NLP to get control back in your own life.

Chapter 8:
Influence and Persuasion

There are many times when the human mind is pretty easy to influence, but it does take a certain set of skills to get people to stop and listen to you. Not everyone is good with influence and persuasion, though. They can talk all day and would not be able to convince others to do what they want. On the other hand, there are those who could persuade anyone to do what they want, even if they had just met this person for the first time. Knowing how to work with these skills will make it easier for you to recognize a manipulator and be better prepared to avoid them if needed.

The first thing that we need to look at is what persuasion is. Persuasion is simply the process or action taken by a person or a group of people when they want to cause something to change. This could be in relation to another human being and something that changes in their inner mental systems or their external behavior patterns.

The act of persuasion, when it is done in the proper way, can sometimes create something new within the person, or it can just modify something that is already present in their minds. There are actually three different parts that come with the process of persuasion including:

- The communicator or other source of the persuasion

- The persuasive nature of the appeal

- The audience or the target person of the appeal

It is important that all three elements are taken into consideration before you try to do any form of persuasion on your own. You can just look around at the people who are in your life, and you will probably be able to see some types of persuasion happening all over the place.

Experts say that people who are good leaders and who have good persuasion powers will utilize the following techniques to help them be successful:

- Exchanging

- Stating

- Legitimizing

- Logical persuasion

- Appealing to value

- Modeling

- Alliance building

- Consulting

- Socializing

- Appealing to a relationship

The above options are all positive ways that you can use persuasion to your advantage. Most people will be amenable to these happening. But on the other side, there are four negative tactics of persuasion that you can do as well. These would include options like manipulating, avoiding, intimidating, and threatening. These negative tactics will be easier for the target to recognize, which is why most manipulators will avoid using them if possible.

Now, you can use some of the tactics above, but according to psychologist Robert Cialdini, there are six major principles of persuasion that can help you to get the results that you want without the target being able to notice what is going on. Let us take a look at these six weapons and how they can be effective.

The six weapons of influence

Reciprocity

The first principle of persuasion that you can use is known as reciprocity. This is based on the idea that when you offer something to someone, they will feel a bit indebted to you and will want to reciprocate it back. Humans are wired to be this way to survive. For the manipulator to use this option, they will make sure that they are doing some kind of favor for their target. Whether that is paying them some compliments, giving them a ride to work, helping out with a big project or getting them out of trouble. Once the favor is done, the target will feel like they owe a debt to the manipulator. The manipulator will then be able to ask for something, and it will be really hard for the target to say no.

Commitment and consistency

It is in the nature of humans to settle for what is already tried and tested in the mind. Most of us have a mental image of who we are and how things should be. And most people are not going to be willing to experiment, so they will keep on acting the way that they did in the past. So, to get them to work with this principle and do what you want, you first need to get them to commit to something. The steps that you would need to follow to get your target to do what you want through commitment and consistency include:

- Start out with something small. You can ask the target to do something small, something that is easier to manage the change, before they start to integrate it more into their personality and get hooked on the habit.

- You can get the target to accept something publicly so that they will feel more obligated to see it through.

- Reward the target when they can stick to the course. Rewards will be able to help strengthen the interest of the target in the course of action that you want them to do.

Social proof

This is another one that will rely on the human tendency, and it relies on the fact that people place a lot of value and trust in other people and in their opinions on things that we have not tried yet. This can be truer if the information comes from a close friend or a person who is perceived as the expert. It is impossible to try out everything in life, and having to rely on others can put us at a disadvantage. This means that we need to find a reliable source to help us get started. A manipulator may be able to get someone to do something by acting as a close friend or an expert. They are able to get the target to try out a course of action because they have positioned themselves as the one who knows the most about the situation or the action.

Likeability

We all know that it is easy to feel attracted to a certain set of people. This can extend to friends and family members as well. So, if you would like to get others to like you and be open to persuasion from you, you first need to figure out how to go from an acquaintance to a friend. This will work similarly to the reciprocity that we talked about earlier, but some of the basic steps that you will need to follow to make this work include:

- *The attraction phase:* You need to make sure that there is something about you that instantly draws the other person to you.

- *Make yourself relatable:* People are more likely to be drawn to you if you are relatable to them in some way. It is also easier to influence another person if they consider you their friend.

- *Communicate like a friend:* Even if the two of you are not quite friends yet, you will be able to make use of the right communication skills so that the target will associate you as a friend.

- *Make it look like you are both in the same groups and that you are fighting for the same causes*: This can make it easier to establish a rapport with them.

Authority

If you want to make sure that you can influence another person, then you need to dress and act the part. This means that you should wear clothes, as well as accessories, that will help you look like you are the one in command. Some of the ways that you can do this include:

- Wear clothes that are befitting to what people will perceive an authoritative figure would wear.

- When you communicate with the target, you need to do so in a commanding fashion.

- Make sure that you can use the lexicon and the language of experts in that field.

When you can position yourself as the authority figure, people will look to you for the answers that they need. It does not matter how well they know you or not. You will have a great opportunity to influence them the way that you want them to behave.

Scarcity

The last weapon that you can use for persuasion is known as scarcity. Humans like the idea of being exclusive and are drawn to anything that they are not necessarily able to find anywhere else. When you make something exclusive, you have a chance of making it appear more valuable. People are also going to become fearful when something they desire starts to disappear. This whole idea is part of the supply and demand principle. If you have something that is abundant, then it will be perceived as having a lower value and cheap. But if it is rare, then it must have a higher value and be more expensive.

This can work for human beings and for products in the same way. Some things that you should keep in mind when you want to use the scarcity principle with persuasion include:

- Always imply that the thing you are offering is not going to be available to the target anywhere else.

- If you can, it is a good idea to implement a countdown timer on what you are offering. This gives a physical indicator to the target that what you are offering is truly going to disappear.

- You should never go back on the stipulations that you said in the beginning. You need to make sure that the target knows that what you offered is scarce, or this method is not going to work very well.

All of these principles can be effective ways for you to be able to use persuasion to manipulate your target. It is important to learn how to use them all and to do so in a covert way so that your target is not able to realize what you are doing. When you are successful with bringing all of this together, you are sure to get the results that you want each time.

Chapter 9:
What if I'm in a Manipulative Relationship?

All manipulative relationships are unbalanced. The only person who is benefitting from this kind of relationship is the manipulator. If you are in this kind of relationship, the manipulator has turned things around so much that they can get you to act and behave in any manner that they want. You may feel that you are not worth the love from someone else. You may always feel worried that you will upset the other person. There may be a lot of guilt-tripping that goes on in the relationship. And even though you keep going because the manipulator is someone you deeply care about, it is very unlikely that the manipulator cares about you at all.

Know your rights

The first thing that you should understand is that you must know your basic rights and know when these rights are being violated. As long as you are not causing harm to others, you have the right to defend and stand up for yourself. The minute you start bringing harm to others, you will automatically forfeit these rights. These basic rights are very important when you are in a relationship. A relationship is a place where you should feel safe and secure with the other person, a place where your basic rights should never be in question. Some of the basic rights that you hold include the right to:

- Express your feelings, wants, and opinions without an outside influence.

- Have your own opinions and beliefs that are different from other people.

- Have others treat you with respect.

- Say no without feeling guilty about it.

- Set your own priorities.

- Be compensated when you pay for something.

- Protect yourself from threats, whether they are emotional, mental, or physical.

- Live a healthy and happy life.

When you are dealing with a manipulator, you will find that you are dealing with a person who has no regard for these rights. They only care about what is important to them, or their own end goals, and they will do whatever it takes to reach these goals, even if it means harming you in the process.

Stay away

This guidebook has taken some time to talk about ways to detect a manipulator before they even get a chance to catch you. You should also keep in mind that a manipulator can act differently depending on the people and situation they are around. They can adapt to the current situation, no matter what it is. Those who are skilled manipulators will be able to be very polite to one person and then rude to another. They may act like they are completely helpless one minute, and then they turn around and become aggressive the next. As soon as you come across a person who can act this way, it is best to avoid all contact with them if possible. You should never decide that you want to change them because they are not going to change. It is always best to just stay away from them as much as possible.

Never give in to the self-blame

Manipulators are good at what they do. They will find and exploit all of your weaknesses. They will make you feel so inadequate that you will start blaming yourself when you are not able to give them what they want. In these scenarios, it is important to remember that you are not the problem and that you have no reason to feel bad about yourself.

Before you fall into the trap of self-blame that the manipulator is trying to push you into, ask yourself these important questions:

- Am I treated with respect?

- Is there a certain amount of give-and-take in the relationship, or am I the only one giving?

- Are the demands of the other person reasonable?

- Am I still happy in this relationship?

The answers that you provide to these questions may be enough to help you realize if you are dealing with a manipulator and that you are not in a healthy relationship.

Ask some more questions

When you are dealing with a manipulator, it is normal that they will make many demands of you, and many of these demands will force you out of your comfort zone. And you will do these things because you want to meet the needs of the manipulator. Most victims are just going to go along with what the manipulator wants because they think this is the only course of action that they have. But it is important to realize that you do have a say. The next time that the manipulator is trying to pressure you into doing something or acting a certain way, consider asking them some questions back, instead of just giving in to what they want. Some questions that you can ask include:

- Do I have any say in this request?

- Does the request sound reasonable to you?

- Are you asking me to do it, or are you demanding that I do it?

- What's in it for me if I do your request?

- Do you think that what you are asking is fair?

- Do you really expect me to....?

When you are asking these questions, you need to be firm. You are using these questions to help you get a deeper sense of the manipulation and where you stand with the other person. If the manipulator has any degree of self-awareness, this is the part where they will back down. But a skilled manipulator who is only after what they want does not care how they harm you. They will just find some excuses and ways to dismiss your questions rather than listening to you.

In addition, you will find that not only do manipulators ask for things that are not reasonable, they also want to get their answers right away. You do not need to respond to them right away. It may make the manipulator upset, but you can tell them that you will think about the request before you do it. Analyze the situation and figure out if you would like to negotiate the request or simply say no to it.

Remember that you always have the right to tell the other person no. You need to stand firm when you tell the other person no. They will try to bully you and get what they want, but if you fight back and stand up for yourself, then you are sure to get the results that you want. The manipulator is not going to want to fight too hard to get what they want, and if you stand firm, they will often back off and leave you alone.

Set the consequences

If you are working with a manipulator who insists on going past your boundaries and will not let you ever say no to them, it is time to set some consequences for this behavior. You can set up the ones that you are comfortable with, but you need to let the manipulator know what these consequences are, and then you need to stick with them when the violation happens. Setting consequences and then going back on them will not stop anything because the manipulator will quickly learn that the consequences are meaningless.

To regain your life after dealing with a manipulator, you need to be ready to take a stand and stand up for yourself. While this may be hard because the manipulator worked to take away a lot of that control to make things easier for themselves, it is so important. Standing up for yourself makes it easier to see your self-worth, and can even make a manipulator back off. Remember that most manipulators want to take the easy course, to find the easy targets that will do what they want without a lot of work or convincing. When you take that away and start to cause some friction

against them, the manipulator is less likely to use their
tactics on you.

Chapter 10:
The Importance of Raising Your Self-Esteem

One of the best things that you can do to fight off manipulation, or to shield yourself from it in the first place, is to learn how to increase your self-esteem. This does not have to be as complicated as you think. But you will find that those who have low self-esteem are the ones who will be taken advantage of in no time. They are the ones who are looking for some approval from their inner voices, the ones who need someone to be there to make them feel better. The manipulator can do this for these people, while also controlling them by being that horrible inner voice.

Someone with a lot of self-esteem is someone who will not fall prey to a manipulator. These people do not need to look outwards to find their self-worth, they can find it within themselves. When a manipulator comes around, they are not going to get very far.

No matter who you are, you can increase your self-esteem. This chapter will take a look at some of the steps that you can take to help improve that self-esteem and keep those manipulators away.

Handle the inner critic

Everyone has an inner critic. Listening to this inner critic can help you to get things done during the day, rather than sitting around and being boring, and it can help you to act in a certain way so that you will gain acceptance from other people. However, if you are not careful with your inner voice, it can kill your self-esteem.

It is pretty normal to have an inner voice that will suggest positive as well as negative thoughts. But, you can determine how those will affect you. Most people will find that when they concentrate on their thoughts, they are dealing with a lot of negativity. This can lower your self-esteem so easily and can make it hard to feel like you are worth much.

You can slowly start to handle that inner critic. Instead of just believing what your inner critic is telling you, it is time to consider whether the information you are thinking is actually true or if it is benefitting you in any way. If not, it is time to throw that negative thought out the window. Focusing on your thoughts and straining out the negative ones can make all the difference in your self-esteem.

A mindset of gratitude

Another thing that you can work on is to learn how to appreciate yourself and all the great things that are in your life. When you are grateful for all the things that you get to enjoy in life, and when you feel good about yourself, your mind will be too full to hold onto those bad and negative thoughts.

You may be surprised to hear it, but most of the suffering you are dealing with in life is completely imaginary. This suffering is created from the dissonance between where you are and where you think you want to be. But where you want to be is a false horizon. If you are not happy with where you are right now and with the journey you are taking, then it is impossible to feel content when you reach the destination.

The trick here is to learn how to be happy in the here and now. You do not have to be exactly where you want to be in life, and this may sound easier said than done, but it is really all that you need to do. If you are too busy thinking about all the things that you are missing out on or how far you are from your goals, it is impossible to have a good amount of self-esteem. A manipulator will see this and take advantage of it right away.

There is always something that you can be thankful for in your life. You can be thankful for the good health you have, the fact that you have a job that pays the bills (even if that job is not that great), friends to hang out with, family, and so much more. If you are not able to find something to be grateful for in your life, it simply means that you are not looking hard enough.

Write things down

You will find that a great way to make sure that you are feeling grateful in your life, and that you are effectively working on your self-esteem, is to start writing things down. Go out and purchase yourself a journal and then spend some time writing down some of your positive traits and the situations that these traits can affect. Do not skimp on this part; you should have a list of at least ten traits that you are proud of and that can help you out.

Then, when you start to feel low or that the day is not going that well, you can take out this list and reread some of these traits. This will instantly improve your mood. You should also take some time to update this list, whether it is once a month, every few months, or even each day.

Another thing that you can do is pick out five things that you are grateful for each day. Do this right away in the morning or at night before you go to bed. You should write down this list and keep it in a place where you can check on it every once in a while. Try to update this list each day, adding in different things (so no copying from the day before). You will be amazed at how many things you can be grateful and happy for in your life.

There is no need to be perfect

In our modern world, it is normal to feel that we need to be perfect all the time. We are in a world of magazines, television shows, and social media that make it seem like everyone else has it together while we are falling apart. Aiming to always be perfect is actually really destructive to your overall thoughts. Perfectionism can actually make it impossible to get things done because you may worry that you are not going to be able to live up to those high standards. And when you do not get the results that you want, either because you did not do it at all, or because you were not able to meet those expectations, then your self-esteem will come crashing down.

The good news is there are some alterations that you can make to your thinking that can help to overcome perfectionism. These include:

- *Strive for good enough:* Instead of aiming for perfectionism, remember that nobody is perfect. It is fine to do a good enough job rather than doing a job to perfection. This takes off a lot of the stress and can make it easier to get things done right.

- *Perfection is only going to harm you:* Life is not like a fairy tale, and you need to learn how to manage your expectations because you are living in the real world. Life will get messy. It will throw you curveballs, you will be tired, and so much more. Things do not always go the way you plan. If you insist on perfectionism, then you will find that it is easy to be disappointed. But if you realize that you live in the real world and that you are doing an amazing job as you are, then you will be able to relax and take things as they come.

Your failures are your lessons

There will be times, no matter how hard you try, that you will make mistakes or that you will fail. The good thing about this happening is that you get to learn a lesson from it. As a perfectionist, you may spend your time trying to avoid these mistakes and then feel horrible when they happen. But this is a horrible idea to have because it will make your self-esteem plummet.

No matter which situation you are in, there is always going to be something positive that you can learn from. It is up to you to figure out what this lesson will be. You should also spend time trying out new things and getting out of your comfort zone whenever you can. When you have new experiences and learn something new, you can feed your confidence and increase your self-esteem.

Never compare to others

This is a hard one to do in our modern world, but the more you compare yourself to other people, the harder it will be to keep your self-esteem up. You are never going to win this game because you will always find someone who is better at something than you are. You need to change this mindset and realize that the only competition that you have in this world is with yourself. It is fine to work to improve on the version of you that you were yesterday, but never to try and improve to who someone else is.

You should always be looking towards the future and figuring out how you can improve your own life. It does not matter what other people are doing. It may seem that they have their lives together and that they are exactly who you want to be. But when it comes down to it, all of us have our flaws and our weaknesses. It is important to find the good in yourself and strive to be a better version of yourself each day, but it is such a waste of time to try and compete with someone else.

Find a good support group

When you find a good support group, one who will be there to cheer you on, pat your back when you are sad, and help you in other ways, then a manipulator does not stand a chance. It is so important that you pay attention to the people you hang around with. If you spend your time with negative people, the ones who complain about how hard their lives are, how unfair things are, and then point out all of the things that you do wrong, how are you supposed to differentiate between them and a skilled manipulator?

These kinds of people will only make it easier for the manipulator to do their job.

It is much better if you can be around people who are positive. These people will be there to lift you up and support you. While you may be stuck with some family members who are downers and who you can't change, you can be in control of your friends and other people you are around. The more positive the people you hang out with, the more they pick you up and cheer you on with your goals, and the better you will be.

Take a look at some of the people you hang out with right now. When you get together with them, do you happen to feel better, more uplifted, when you are all done? Or do you feel like they brought you down some more and like you are drained out after the meeting? If you feel the latter, then you are hanging out with the wrong group of people, and it is time to go and find a new support group that will lift you up and is there for you no matter what you are going through.

There are a lot of places you can go to find the right support group for your needs. You can join a group that holds the same interests as you, go to church, go to some events, join a mom's group if you have kids, take some classes at the local school, and so much more. As soon as you start to look for this positive support group, you will be amazed at how many places you will be able to run into the right kinds of people.

Working on your self-esteem is something that will take some time to accomplish. You may have been dealing with low self-esteem for a long time, and changing things around so you feel more positive will not happen overnight. Learning how to avoid that negative voice that is in your head, how to stop comparing yourself to others, and finding the right support group can all make a large difference in your self-esteem. The higher you can get that self-esteem, the easier it is to scare those manipulators away.

Conclusion

Thank you for making it through to the end of this book, let's hope it was informative and was able to provide you with all the tools you need to achieve your goals.

The next step is to start to use the information that is found in this guidebook to help you out when manipulation strikes or to manipulate a situation in a way that benefits you. There are times in our lives when we are manipulated by those around us and when we choose to manipulate others. And as long as it is on occasion, and for simple things that do not really harm other people (such as trying to get someone to give us a ride home), it can be socially acceptable.

Finally, if you found this book useful in any way, a review on Amazon is always appreciated!